# INITIATIONS
## ON THE PATH OF THE SOUL

# Initiations

## ON THE PATH
## OF THE SOUL

WHITE EAGLE

THE WHITE EAGLE PUBLISHING TRUST
NEW LANDS · LISS · HAMPSHIRE · ENGLAND
www.whiteaglepublishing.org

Published as THE PATH OF THE SOUL, September 1959
Second edition, revised and expanded, December 1997
First published under the present title, July 2007

© Copyright, The White Eagle Publishing Trust,
1959, 1997, 2007

British Library Cataloguing-in-Publication Data
A catalogue record for this book is available from the
British Library

ISBN 978-0-85487-183-4

Chapter decorations by Rosemary Young

Set in 13 on 15 point Monotype Perpetua
Printed and bound in Sri Lanka by
Universal Packaging (Pty) Ltd,
77 Nungamugoda Rd, Kelaniya

# CONTENTS

# Introduction: the Path of the Soul

T he teaching in this book describes the course of human life in terms of progressive initiation into inner or higher wisdom, following a symbolic pattern of birth, baptism, temptation, transfiguration, crucifixion and resurrection; and it was given in the following circumstances. White Eagle, the spirit guide of Grace Cooke and the being under whose guidance the White Eagle Lodge was founded, had given at the Lodge's London premises, during the last months of the second world war, a series of teachings describing the inner meaning of St John's gospel. The communication had been much enhanced by a vision Grace Cooke had had of St John, the beloved disciple of Jesus, at an Albigensian castle in the foothills of the Pyrenees in 1931. Those teachings have since been reprinted, along with the story of the vision and other White Eagle material on the theme of the gospel, in the book THE LIVING WORD OF ST JOHN (published by the White Eagle Publishing Trust in 1949 and now in its third edition, 2000). In that book, White Eagle defines 'soul' in the following way. He describes first how God created man–woman in His–Her own image and breathed into this new creation the breath of life (Genesis 1 : 2). Thus man–woman became a living soul. He continues:

*Confusion still exists concerning the nature and functions of the soul and also of the spirit of man. Once spirit comes down to dwell in the flesh it starts to create what is called a soul, for soul is that part of man's being which is built up through experiences undergone by the tender inner self of man during incarnation. Soul can be further described as the feminine aspect of man's life, the mother-principle ... the first principle being divine will, the father or masculine aspect.*

This passage is repeated here because it helps to explain the title of the present volume. The discussion on soul and spirit is continued and complemented in the last chapter of this book. The 'path of the soul' is, fully, the path of the spirit, which first separates from the Oneness of God so that it may grow through seemingly independent existence (in fact, it is never really separated, but undergoes the illusion of doing so). In so-called separation it acquires about it a soul, a receptive aspect to its being, which takes in all the richness of remembered experience. It learns to find love, even though the world at first seems not to be full of it. Thus 'the path of the soul' is precisely the experience that every one of us goes through, whether or not we are conscious of doing so: the experience of having to go through doubt about the love that pervades all life, and then through spiritual growth finding it again. The optimism, or rather the faith behind White Eagle's teaching, is that the path of the soul takes us back to, not away from, the Godhead, the Oneness, but with a hugely greater consciousness and joy. We believe theefore that this is a book which will lead to greater happiness as well as understanding.

Nonetheless, it seems worth recording in this introduction the words with which White Eagle began this set of teachings, describing the sort of attention that he felt they demanded in the listener or reader. He said:

*We welcome all our brethren to this group. We have one or two serious things to say at the beginning of this new session [the Lodge had been closed for the month of August, and White Eagle was speaking on 12th September 1945].We know that there are those who can only visit these gatherings intermittently, but as everything said here is recorded, it is possible for those who cannot attend regularly to obtain records of subsequent meetings.*

*To all who are serious in their study and in their*

*aspirations towards truth we would say, 'Do not come to these groups lightly or out of curiosity'. Perhaps some fault in ourselves may fail to hold your attention and your interest. If this be so, we ask for your kindness and sympathy. It is not always possible to bring through the higher truths which we would like. According to the vibrations of the earth and the astrological vibration there is a swing of the pendulum. Sometimes we would sweep up to the heavens; at other times it is not possible. But we would point out that even on the lower levels of consciousness there is much to be learned. Not always by soaring into the heaven-world is truth recorded. Truth comes through the soul's perception of love.*

As originally given, the present talks were interspersed with passages from St Matthew's and St Luke's gospels in the same way as the series printed in THE LIVING WORD OF ST JOHN referred to St John's. Yet White Eagle's account of the life of Jesus is so hugely indebted to the mysticism with which St John treats it that even when White Eagle quotes from the other gospels, it is almost as though he is reading the material through St John's eyes. This closeness is ever real. The traditional use of the eagle as St John's symbol is, it would seem, scarcely coincidence.

When this book was re-edited for the edition of 1997, a few other passages were found that had not been reproduced in the first edition. Today, with public awareness of spirit teaching having developed, it seems absolutely right to put them in, and the result is that the book is slightly longer, and accordingly richer.

Our other desire in preparing a new edition of THE PATH OF THE SOUL, and particularly the edition under the new title (2007) was to keep abreast of changes in English usage which render some of the terms of the old text anachronistic. When White Eagle gave his talks, the impersonal use of the word 'man' and all the terms dependent upon it was read without question as including both sexes. Yet the whole tenor of White Eagle's teaching is to stress that God is both Father and Mother and that every human being has within them elements of masculine and feminine. In this edition we are pleased that it has been possible to make small, but significant changes to remove virtually all of the gender-specific words. However, the words 'brotherhood' and 'brethren' have virtually no alternatives that we can think of without limiting the full sense, so we have left them. Language is today at a transitional stage: in some ways it is much easier to speak inclusively of both genders, in other ways much more cumbersome. In preparing this text we have tried as far as possible, without distorting the meaning in any way, to use the opportunities contemporary usage provides for inclusiveness. We have updated a few other terms in the process.

Originally, each of the talks began with a prayer of invocation. We have kept one at the beginning and one at the end.

# 1 · The Preparation

*W*E RAISE *our hearts to the beloved Father–*
*Mother and to the Son. We praise Thee and*
*give thanks. We pray in spirit for communion*
*with Thee, and for the expansion and growth of Thy spirit, Thy*
*wisdom and Thy love in our being....*

You may wonder why we refer so often to the gospel of
St John. We have done so because this gospel contains
the truth of spiritual unfoldment from the beginning
to the end. The more one ponders over the writings
of St John, the deeper one goes into the Ancient Wisdom and into a knowledge which every living soul is
consciously or unconsciously seeking. This knowledge
can unveil the nature of life in the heaven worlds and
also give new understanding of the value of every
detail and happening which goes to make up everyday

life. It is not only the vision glorious that you need to sustain you, but also the power and wisdom to bring such knowledge through into your life on earth. Your life should then become so directed and influenced by it that this knowledge radiates not only through your character but through the physical body itself.

If you study the gospel of St John with increasing understanding, if you can attune yourself so that you automatically express or manifest something of divine truth in daily life, then you will be preparing yourself for the supreme initiation. Some people think that initiation involves going through a ceremony of some kind, and this in a sense is true, as far as the outer plane is concerned. The initiation we have in mind, however, is something which is taking place every day throughout life.

The soul in incarnation may endeavour to put into practice the spiritual truth which it has acquired through meditation, in which case it will prepare itself through initiation after initiation. Or, as is so often the case, the being will remain unaware, wrapped up in its earthly self and be 'spiritually dead', or *know not anything*, as the Bible says. The spiritually dead cannot comprehend, cannot absorb, cannot even glimpse truth. They live in a state of darkness. So we have these two, those who know and those who do not know: those who have perceived reality, and those who are still blind to the real life. By absorbing the words of the great teacher recorded in the gospel of St John the soul can recognize what is happening as it passes step by step through initiations on the various planes of life. Yet some people cling to the idea that initiation can come about only by recognized stages—say, by attaining to what is called the first, second, third, or fourth, or even the thirty-third degree. This is not always so; if you search your own inner experience, you may find that you have been preparing for a number of degrees at the same time, but are not yet complete in any one of them. In other words, you are training on one level for a period and then on another; so we find that the soul, through contact with its brothers and sisters, and through all the experiences of its incarnation, is preparing throughout human life for the supreme initiation. This we know as the Christ initiation, or initiation into the full power and consciousness of the divine, the Christ light, which is called the Son of God.

The life of Jesus the Christ as pictured in the gospels is also the story of the life of every soul. It presents the story of the major spiritual experiences which will await every pupil who seeks knowledge and wisdom, and who will in turn pass through all the temptations and even endure crucifixion and resurrection, for these experiences can take many different forms. This you should bear in mind whenever you study and meditate upon the four gospels, and particularly that of St John. Religions throughout all time have presented this esoteric knowledge concerning the soul's birth or descent into matter, its experiences through living imprisoned in the flesh, and its arising from matter—or through its being raised from the 'floor' into the 'chair': into the place of command, or mastership.

All religions teach these truths according to the understanding of their adherents. Some of this teaching may appear crude or at least elementary. This is because the inner truth has vanished and only the shell has been retained. Only the earnest seeker can still descend into the vault and dig, and there uncover spiritual treasure. But to obtain this treasure demands far more than mere exercise of intellect. Not by intellectual powers alone are these mysteries uncovered, but through daily practice of the presence of God. This may sound obvious; you may have heard it often before. Yet when the soul absorbs the divine light through constant meditation upon the light, and through opening the heart in compassion, tenderness and love towards all life, then the veil is drawn aside, and the soul *becomes* truth, *becomes* light; and this light within the soul never again departs from it.

Some of your own personal experiences have already proved this to be true. For when carried away by joy or overwrought by pain, or at any time when you are emotionally over-stressed, you are like a frail boat tossed about in a storm. Yet within everyone awaits the sleeping Master, the indwelling Christ. When at last you call upon Him in your distress, crying, 'Master, help me!' you are appealing not to any outside teacher but to the Christ within. You cry, 'O Thou who are light and power and love, come to my aid!' Then tranquillity steals over you. You are at last aware of an indwelling strength and you become still. Perhaps later, when you have trained yourself in meditation, you can feel yourself rise as on a shaft of light at this time. You then have power to function on a plane superior to this and, looking down upon your emotional disturbance, you will see it for what it really is.

This control over emotion, anger and fear is one of the earliest degrees of initiation—not by repression but by sublimation of these emotions, which can be seen by the clairvoyant as tongues of flame darting through the aura. All the unruly emotions can be subdued and transmuted by the Christ within, and any passion that has been aroused, instead of injuring and destroy-ing—for it *can* destroy—goes forth instead with power to heal, to bless, to lighten the burdens of the world, manifesting amid the darkness as pure white light.

Nothing causes a more severe reaction upon the physical body than violent emotion. You may not always recognize this as a real cause of subsequent illness; you suffer bodily pain, and you attribute it to a physical origin. The aspirant on the path, however, must be prepared to acknowledge truth. Emotions which can shatter your finer bodies eventually cause ill-health, to a greater or a lesser extent. Therefore control of the emotional body, and the transmutation of all the lower passions into the higher, is certain to have an enormous effect upon the health. The soul which lives close to the Christ light usually has a harmonious and healthy body.

Here we must add that nobody, whether discarnate or incarnate, can judge the soul of another. Indeed, no initiate would dare to judge, but would simply give forth love and healing from his or her own aura to the person concerned, without criticism or question, though perhaps offering a word of advice. The initiate well understands that a human being can only go forward step by step, learning by trial and error, gradually acquiring wisdom, self-control and spiritual illumination. Even so, often when the soul appears to be almost perfect there is something left which has not been transmuted, and this may manifest in some bodily disease, however slight. The soul must acquire complete dispassion. We mean it must meet every event of human life with tranquillity, knowing that everything which happens results either from its own previous failure or achievement, and that all works together for good.

We may dislike it! We may exclaim, 'This sorrow will

break me! How can a God of love send me these things?'
But God's love is so much greater than our human conception of love, and God sends these happenings into
human life in order to give the soul an opportunity to
strengthen itself and to meet all the experiences of life
with tranquillity of spirit, never doubting that whatever
happens is for its eventual good.

The Bible records many stories of individuals who
were tested, seemingly almost beyond endurance, but
who came through. Such a one was Job, who underwent
all kinds of sorrows until everything was taken from
him. Even his body was a mass of festering sores, but
he still held fast to the love of God, and so he passed
the test. He knew that whatever happened was either
because he had deserved it, or was something which
had come to test him for his final initiation.

From this instance and others which could be cited
you may gather that the great and advanced soul keeps
true to its awareness that God is altogether good. God
sends human beings sufferings only out of love. Indeed,
only through undergoing such experiences can the soul
find strength, and only through practice learn to stand
unmoved. My brethren, as we talk you can feel that
inner poise come, that inner strength which inspires in
you the greatest courage. You then know that nothing
has power to destroy the eternal love, the living flame
within; that nothing matters much so long as you know

God or Christ within you. The Bible bids us lay up our treasure in heaven (Matthew 6 : 20), in the assurance that when the soul grows rich within, it becomes possessed of priceless wealth that nothing can destroy or take away.

Now, step by step, we shall amplify these teachings concerning the soul's awakening, the soul's initiation. We shall see how closely these are related not only to the Christian doctrine but also to other religions throughout the ages—realizing that this is indeed the Ancient Wisdom, the jewel of truth possessing many facets. At the same time we would emphasize that this knowledge is of very little use if the aspirant only becomes engrossed intellectually; there must come a realization of the light which burns within and a *becoming* of that light.

# 2 · The Water Initiation: I

W E COME from the spiritual realms to try to impart some of the knowledge which we ourselves have found. We cannot travel your path, or live your life for you, but we can act as a signpost, and tell you from our own experience where that path will lead. The freewill choice as to the direction you follow will still be yours, for you have to learn to develop and use the qualities of discernment and discrimination. One thing, however, is quite certain: truth can only be discerned from the innermost, from the pure spirit. This is why the Master so clearly advised his followers to become 'as little children', which means to draw aside from the promptings of the earthly or reasoning mind. You will say, 'But surely our reason is given to us to use?' Yes, your reason has its own special purpose, but it cannot enable you to discern spiritual truth. Spiritual truth, when revealed to the vision of the spirit by the Christ within, will pass the most searching test of reason, for being complete and unanswerable it satisfies all the yearnings of your being.

We are now going to deal specifically with the first of the initiations which the soul has to undergo. It is the Water Initiation, called by some 'baptism by water'. By this we do not mean the baptism of infants as is customary in a church, but what we may call 'soul baptism'. We would begin by explaining that a baptism or cleansing by water is customary when the soul first leaves the physical. When you go into meditation you may be confronted by a bathing pool or lake of blue water. Coming from the harsh and turbulent conditions of earth, the soul on entering the higher planes has need of being purified before it can proceed further, and so it is thus cleansed.

For the symbolism is not only of the water which cleanses; it is the human soul itself which is signified by the water element. In the Bible and also in other mystical revelations 'the waters' signify the psyche, the soul. There is water that is still and calm and which will reflect truth, and there is water that is so rough that it reflects nothing. So the soul qualities of the individual have to be brought under control by the Master. Before a soul can proceed on the path of initiation, the Christ within must discipline that soul and make it calm enough to reflect the true image of the higher worlds. This was the first initiation undergone by Jesus. You ask, 'But why did such a being as Jesus need any kind of initiation—surely He was beyond our limitations?' But Jesus the Christ was also Jesus the man, and therefore had to undergo exactly the same training and follow the same path that all must follow. But remember also that although true in itself this story is also an allegory depicting the life of every soul. Every soul must eventually be 'baptized' or cleansed emotionally. Again, we do not refer to the ceremony of baptism in any church: we are speaking of certain inner experiences which await every soul.

If you read the account of John the Baptist in the gospels, you will notice that the place in which he dwelt is described as a wilderness—the wilderness of the world, the chaotic condition of the human soul. We are all in a wilderness within until we begin to discipline ourselves and turn our soul wilderness into a beautiful garden. The term 'wilderness' in fact stands for the state of chaos, loneliness and unhappiness which is the lot of the soul before it is awakened.

The meaning of the name John is 'the gift of God'. God sends to the human soul the gift of a teacher. When the soul is ready to be baptized, the teacher is there, to show the soul what it longs to know; thus John, the gift of God, was ready to teach those who came to be cleansed and purified (Matthew 3 : 5–6).

Note also the description of John's raiment and the way he lived, for this too has an inner meaning. The soul who wants to learn must be clothed with humility, and be prepared to eat very simple food. Some are not satisfied unless they have an intellectual feast put before them. They eat grossly and suffer afterwards. Having swallowed, in a mental and spiritual sense, more than they can stomach, they later turn away in discomfort from their spiritual aspiration. By contrast, the true aspirant is clothed with humility, and prepared to nurture his or her spirit upon simple foods.

John is said to have called his people to repent, but what *is* repentance? Does it mean no more than saying, 'Oh, I am sorry', promising that such a thing will not happen again, and afterwards doing exactly the same—as we all do, many, many times? No: repentance means real effort and real determination to change oneself and not again miss the mark. What does 'sin' mean? We would say that sin is a failure to go direct to the truth. When striking out his first furrow across a field a ploughman has always to keep his eye fixed upon a distant marking-post. If his eye wanders he cannot drive a straight furrow. This applies also to our own actions, particularly to our relations with one another. We 'sin' when we fail to drive a straight furrow to the marking-post. Some people may protest that they have kept the Ten Commandments, and how can they then have sinner? The answer is that every time the soul does not live truth from its innermost being, it is sinning. Sin is not of the body only—indeed, the bodily sins we would not call sins at all. Sin is the failure of the soul to live truly, to express truth in thought and word and deed.

Always to be true is most difficult. Nevertheless, whenever a soul fails to be true, it is guilty of sin; so we begin to see how many of us are sinners, simply through weakness or sloth.

*And Jesus, when he was baptized, went up straightway out of the water: and, lo, the heavens were opened unto him, and he saw the Spirit of God descending like a dove, and lighting upon him: and lo, a voice from heaven, saying, This is my beloved Son, in whom I am well pleased.*

(Matthew 3 : 16–17)

Now, when the soul has been mystically baptized, it has passed the Water Initiation, which means that it has become disciplined and no longer gives way to anger, fear, or passion. Having undergone its test, it has learned how to remain tranquil. It has overcome all hasty judgments, all angry passion, all subtle fear and anxiety. In this state the soul is at last able to see the vision and hear the voice of God. How could it hope to hear before, when it was making too much noise within itself? But when at last it becomes like a calm lake shining beneath the sun or moon, then the heavens reflect their glory in the waters of the soul. Thus the soul, when in meditation, reflects the heavens: a true, not a false reflection (as is frequently the case when there is mental and emotional disturbance, and the psychic feelings are all astir).

This is where messages of a purely psychic origin can go wrong. You may be dismayed, not realizing that the distortion is the result of your own inner disturbances. But you will realize that disappointments of this nature are ultimately good because they test the sincerity and earnestness of the soul. If the soul is not truly treading the path, it does not make any progress. However, if it is true to itself, the soul is not dismayed but keeps on striving for spiritual truth, learning how to discipline itself. At last, when the soul is dispassionate, calm and tranquil, it hears the inner voice. How does the soul hear? The innermost soul *knows* in a flash such an interchange of spiritual power from God, the source of its being, that it can afterwards say in the face of all unbelief, 'I know because quite truly I have heard the voice of God speak. Nothing can ever shake or alter me after this experience'.

As the soul learns to overcome its turbulent emotions, to live tranquilly, kindly, lovingly, then as a result the physical body housing the soul should become in due time healthy and indeed perfect. We may touch upon rather a sensitive spot here because many people su er more or less from ill-health; the body is rarely the perfect expression of the Christ within. But how many people realize that undisciplined and uncontrolled emotions disturb their bloodstream and glandular system, and that this eventually produces minor, and later perhaps major, ailments? Of course this should not happen. After the Water Initiation has been passed, the soul can live calmly, patiently and happily day by day: unperturbed and undisturbed, reflecting only the heavenly, the true conditions of the God-life. In course of time it will be able to express through the body its own perfect wholeness or healthfulness.

So if you are at present sick in body or mind, take heart from what we say, and try to understand, try to absorb this one simple truth; and know that there is always a tomorrow, always a fresh opportunity waiting. Endeavour to attune all your higher bodies harmoniously to the spiritual law, and presently there will be recreated for you a new and perfect body, reborn from the harmony of the Christ within.

# 3 · The Water Initiation: II

S OMETIMES when we open our hearts in prayer, we pray that we may lay down our burdens and enter heaven. But to lay down a burden does not mean to shed responsibility. Responsibility, if looked at in the right way, should not be a burden but rather an opportunity or even a joy; because while we are tested by our responsibilities we also earn them, and as the soul matures it becomes capable of undertaking more important tasks. If you could only realize it, the responsibilities that come to you are also your opportunities for service.

Some people want to rid themselves of their responsibilities, and others take on unnecessary burdens and regard them as responsibilities. But we must learn to discriminate between the two. Do not the burdens and cares which weigh us down exist because we ourselves are in darkness, and do not understand the love, the power or the wisdom of God? Everything in life can become a burden, instead of being part of that joy which our life should be. So when we say, 'Let us lay down our burdens', the words really mean the laying down of unnecessary fears, anxieties and tortures which come through the soul's conflict with others, and with the conditions of its own life. When we can see where we are going, when we have realized the power, the love and the wisdom of God, we carry our burdens no longer. So we want to learn more about these attributes of God, for when we really understand the spiritual life we are filled with light, which means lightness: we shall not carry burdens then.

To illustrate this for yourselves, think for one moment of leaving aside all material things, and entering into tranquillity and peace. As soon as you touch the vibration of tranquillity and calmness you have no burdens. They have fallen away, because you have entered into an *illumined* consciousness. When you know God, your soul will be filled with the radiance of God, it will be *anointed*, and you will be able to meet all the situations of everyday life with complete tranquillity.

We speak of this because where the Bible describes the anointing of Jesus, it means that Jesus the mortal man, Jesus the prophet, Jesus the teacher, was anointed by the spirit of Christ entering into or taking possession of him at that moment. We have previously discussed the baptism and explained that the experiences of Jesus the Master are identical with the experiences through which every human soul will eventually pass. We shall try presently to compare these with some of your own soul experiences and with those of every soul endeavouring to tread the path.

In course of time we shall all have to pass through four main initiations. Every human soul reincarnates according to its needs, and each mortal life offers the soul its opportunity to undergo one or other of these four initiations.

At the moment we are still concerned with the Water Initiation, appertaining to the soul's desires, feelings or emotions—the psyche. This initiation is indeed one with which all those sensitive enough to touch the psychic realms are faced, and lies before all souls striving to overcome desire within their nature. Desire can manifest on every plane of one's being, physical, mental and spiritual; and the work of the candidate is not necessarily to erase these feelings, emotions, and desires, but to gain full control over them.

We are told that Jesus was called to the river Jordan to be baptized. You are all called to a river Jordan to undergo its 'baptism'. Certain religious sects believe that by actual immersion of the body in water something happens to the soul. This is true; but baptism really means that cleansing and purification which takes place when the soul feels 'called to Jordan' (or to the place of true repentance) when the soul feels at last that it must find God. The soul of Jesus, which was now age-old, already knew consciously many things. As we have said before, every soul that reincarnates has to face these same tests, but having been tested in former lives, as Jesus had, it remembers and is strong. After the first, the initiations are therefore simple.

Jesus heard the voice of God saying, *This is my beloved Son, in whom I am well pleased* (Matthew 3 : 17). Surely others also hear this voice in their own souls and are overcome with emotion or raised to a pitch of awareness? You as well as we have at some time had some wonderful spiritual experience and been raised to a state of joy and ecstasy? Perhaps this has come to you in the form of an actual communication with some loved one who has passed on, or during a religious service, or when listening to beautiful music—some outstanding, uplifting experience which has awoken you to the presence and the glory of God. How wonderful are the ways of the spirit! How glorious is God! Emotion overwhelms you. You feel that you have at last found your salvation.

The soul when thus deeply moved has literally heard the voice of God. You feel that you will never again look back. All is well; you have entered your spiritual home, your Lodge. But something comes after: when these wonders have been seen and heard, the testing follows. Everyone goes through this testing. Indeed, after the first arising of the spirit a whole series of tests awaits every soul on its path.

When this testing comes, some become disillusioned and think that all they believed to be true is wrong. Others are not so easily shaken, and though they may be perplexed and puzzled, they hold fast to the belief that they have both seen and heard the truth. They keep on keeping on.

Others again become disappointed with those they contact as they go about the world. People are only too ready to say, 'Well, fancy So-and-So, while professing religion, behaving like that!', while forgetting that their companion is walking the selfsame path as they are and needs compassionate understanding and sympathy when he or she fails. *Judge not, that ye be not judged* (Matthew 7 : 1). We cannot, we dare not judge anyone. We are all moving forward on the same path, and while our brother or sister may fall below the standard sometimes, so do we. What treatment shall we expect when our turn comes to fall? Think what it would mean to us were our brother or sister to come to us then and say, 'Never mind; let us forget what happened. Let me help you to rise, brother, and carry on'. This is the way, the truth, and the life.

We are told that Jesus, having received the call, went away into the wilderness: in a sense, into the world. All aspirants, after hearing a similar call, have to return to take up their mortal life again and wander in the wilderness of the world. They want to be good, they try to hold fast to God and to the vision they have seen; but the world is so difficult and people are so difficult, and the aspirant is apt to look with despair at his or her particular part of the wilderness. You look at the world at the present time and think: 'O dear, this is hopeless!'. The mists and illusions of the material world befog you. Nevertheless you are there to learn something. That something is to hold fast to the Christ within yourself. Only when this Christ-power becomes deeply established within can the candidate be called anointed.

Try not to think in terms of days, weeks or years, or about any particular period of time, but rather in terms of many incarnations; the way of the spirit is very sure, and slow and mysterious. Tests can be long continued, for the soul is intended to become very resolute in itself, very firmly established in the light of the spirit. It has to turn continually inwards to the strength of its own inner spirit, of the Christ within. At every twist of the road, before every difficulty and problem confronting it, the soul must learn to hold fast to that inner light.

Jesus wandered in the wilderness for forty days. The Israelites dwelt for forty years in the wilderness. There are many references in the Bible to the number forty. We think that the use of this number originates from the period that a babe is carried in its mother's womb, roughly forty weeks; forty therefore symbolizes a time of confinement and limitation. The soul, after hearing the voice of God saying, 'This is my beloved Son–Daughter', then goes through tests and trials arising out of its own limitation. You will know the feeling. If you have once seen heaven revealed, if only for a moment, and heard the voice of the spirit, you will understand. So great is the wonder that many people complain afterwards, 'Why have I to linger on in this old body? I wish I could be set free from it for ever', not realizing that they would not be out of their particular wood even then. Far from it! All is not glory in the spirit world unless a soul has the light shining within itself. All will depend on the quality of that soul, upon its present-day reactions when it faces up to conditions which seem very hard to hear, or is being tempted by Satan—meaning by this Saturn, the planet which brings limitation. Yet you may be thankful for the influence of Saturn, for through the limitations and testings which it bring the soul grows strong and rich.

Let us read and ponder over the three temptations of Jesus, and try to associate them with our own personal experience, seeing how far they offer an explanation.

> *Then was Jesus led up of the Spirit into the wilderness*
> *to be tempted of the devil. And when he had fasted forty*
> *days and forty nights, he was afterward an hungred. And*
> *when the tempter came to him, he said, If thou be the*
> *Son of God, command that these stones be made bread.*
> *But he answered and said, It is written, Man shall not*
> *live by bread alone, but by every word that proceedeth*
> *out of the mouth of God.*

(Matthew 4 : 1–4)

*He was afterward an hungred* [i.e., hungry]. The body of
Jesus, we learn, after this fast of forty days longed for
food. There is, of course, one interpretation, given on
the outer plane, which is the temptation which can assail
every soul which has gained power to perform miracles
for its own satisfaction—a thing which the Christ or the
person of true spirit will never do. However great their
capacity, they will never use it for themselves. Another
interpretation is that when the soul has once seen the
light, it longs for physical manifestation. People who
are seeking the spirit world say, 'If only I could hear
the actual voice of my loved one with my own ears,
or see the form with my own eyes, or really touch
my loved one, I should be satisfied ever after'. That is
another way of wanting to turn stones into bread. But

even then the Christ within says, 'No, you should not live for physical manifestation alone, but by the Word of God, the spirit of God, by the inner knowledge of God'. The aspirant learns to deny any promptings to use the Christ-power, the power of God, in order to satisfy himself or herself.

The soul truly on the path remains absolutely un-perturbed by any of these hammerings of the lower self. It does not want anything like that, for it needs only to realize the light of God and hold fast to that inner knowledge, that inner light. It wants no outward manifestations at all. Yet these are still a big temptation. Fasting, bodily purification, both these will help, and are good if they also imply that the *mind* becomes clean and wholesome. Nevertheless it is not so much what a person eats as what they think, what they are in their inner self, that purifies them. Let them by all means abstain from things which are unclean, by which we mean that which is innately unholy, unhealthy, unwor-thy. Fasting really means living in a state of purity. Of course, when a person's mind and soul are pure because they have learned to abstain, the body no longer desires to eat anything which savours of cruelty, which is surely unholy and unhealthy.

*Then the devil taketh him up into the holy city, and setteth him on a pinnacle of the temple, And saith unto*

> him, *If thou be the Son of God, cast thyself down: for it is written, He shall give his angels charge concerning thee: and in their hands they shall bear thee up, lest at any time thou dash thy foot against a stone. Jesus saith unto him, It is written again, Thou shalt not tempt the Lord thy God.*

(Matthew 4 : 5–7)

Notice that *the devil taketh him up into the holy city,* the city of Jerusalem, to tempt him. Jerusalem means a centre of peace. When the soul enters 'Jerusalem' it means that it has found the place of peace. Yet if it is too sure of itself, the tempter within says, 'Why should *I* need to depend on God for everything? I can now do anything I like, having passed my test, my initiation. Now I can remain here indefinitely. No harm can befall my body or my soul. At last I am safe. Why then should I still continue to discipline myself?' You know the kind of argument which goes on in the soul, particularly after it has travelled a little way on the path? Then the Christ within arises and says, *'Thou shalt not tempt the Lord thy God.* You must continue to strive after the perfect way, continue to be true to me. Beware of breaking the spiritual laws of God'. This particular temptation originates from pride, in which there is usually a degree of ignorance.

There is also another interpretation. Some people

are inclined to use their spiritual knowledge for their own ends, thinking that by sending out a sufficiently powerful thought they can attract anything they like to themselves—which is true. Send out a thought and you can draw material things to you. But this is not the way of the initiate. It is for him or her to overcome this particular temptation. They must depend purely and simply upon the spirit of God, saying, 'Thy will, O God, not mine!' It really means surrender of the soul to the divine spirit, so that the soul does not try to use spiritual power to gain anything for itself, but lives sweetly and purely in the Christ light.

*Again, the devil taketh him up into an exceeding high mountain, and sheweth him all the kingdoms of the world, and the glory of them; and saith unto him, All these things will I give thee, if thou wilt fall down and worship me. Then saith Jesus unto him, Get thee hence, Satan: for it is written, Thou shalt worship the Lord thy God, and him only shalt thou serve. Then the devil leaveth him, and behold, angels came and ministered unto him.*

(Matthew 4 : 8–11)

Many successful people—the religiously-minded as well as the materially-minded—are tempted to believe that their success is entirely due to themselves. They think how clever they are! They forget that without the help and blessing of God nothing can ever be accomplished. Not through men and women alone but by the will of God do conditions arise in human life destined to give the soul opportunities to serve God. Many worldly people become intoxicated with their own material success, and this can also happen on the spiritual path. People can become charged with spiritual pride, inwardly thinking how good they are and how nice they are to know! They have indeed been carried up into a high mountain: to a place of high consciousness, that is what it means. When the soul is thus raised, the tempter, which is the lower self, now whispers, 'How wonderful I am! It is I who have attained this spiritual height. I have made this great progress—all by myself!' But the soul who would triumph over these three temptations must know that whatever it achieves spiritually, it is of itself nothing and can do nothing; and that all the good that is in it is of God.

These temptations shrewdly come to test how strong is Christ within. For Christ speaking and acting in the soul is humble, pure, loving and gentle, ever meek and kind, wishing no evil and knowing no wrong, keeping on and on labouring in humility and love, and therefore growing very strong. This, then, is the purpose of Saturn or Satan, limiting and tempting us in our wilderness, to teach us to depend upon the gentle Christ within.

Whatever your problem, whatever your hardship or difficulty, turn within; you will surely find your answer. Light will be shed upon your path. Have courage to face the truth, and you will then pass the Water Initiation, and will become firmly established as an initiate, as a master of the water element: the psychic, the emotional element in yourself. You can then create your heaven upon earth.

Seek God first—only God. As you seek you shall find.

# 4 · The Proof in Life

W E HAVE dealt with the three particular temptations every aspirant for the Water Initiation has to undergo, and having triumphed over them, return to his or her appointed place in life. There they are filled with the power of the spirit and with desire to share with others the truth that they have found. But how does the soul preach this wonderful gospel of truth? Already there are many, many people who by writing and talking are endeavouring to induce others to accept their beliefs. But truth is of the spirit, and cannot be conveyed by words alone. The initiate has to become a power in daily life so that without preaching, and often without even speaking, but by the emanation of the soul he or she teaches the gospel of truth, conveying truth to others by the measure of the Christ-spirit within.

*By their fruits ye shall know them* (Matthew 7 : 20). This means by the manifestation of the spirit of Christ, the radiance given forth by the soul. From some people you can receive a great deal without a word being spoken. Such individuals are often retiring and are certainly humble, gentle and tender with others, but have within them the power of the spirit which they are continually giving out to heal the sick in mind and body, to comfort the mourner and raise those who are downcast in spirit.

They are also giving true riches to the poor. *Blessed are the poor in spirit,* Jesus said (Matthew 5 : 3). Who are these poor in spirit? They are those who have reached a stage in their spiritual development where they are ready both to receive and absorb truth and light from an initiate. One who has passed through the Water Initiation, which means one who has learned to control emotion, who can distinguish between what is real and what is unreal: such a one is radiating true power, spiritual light, and Christlikeness. The one poor in spirit is the soul ready to absorb the radiance of the soul of the initiate. *Blessed are they.*

Yet there are many, many souls who are not yet ready; who scoff at spiritual truth and are interested only in their business or the things of this world, and who, because they do not want to hear, have not yet earned the title 'poor in spirit'. The poor in spirit are able to recognize God, they see God shining through the water initiate. The initiate is able to heal the sick. Power is given to him or her. Again it is not always by words. At night when the body is asleep the soul of such a one goes forth. When you desire to heal the sick, or to give comfort to the lonely, if you will meditate upon this act of healing before you go to sleep you will leave your body in sleep in the same way. Although you will not be conscious of it, the light of the Christ in your soul will be imparted to the sick one and it will be this light which will heal.

We think that there are a great many people today who have unknowingly reached the stage of being 'poor in spirit'. If so, they all have a great work before them, not necessarily to be accomplished by teaching or preaching from a platform or pulpit, but by putting the power of Christ into their everyday life. With Christ anything can be accomplished; the mistake that so many people make is to depend on their own power. For the secret is to enter the heart chamber, the inner self, the place of tranquillity and stillness, and there pray; in other words, to stand on one side and let the God-power work through the medium of the body, mind and soul. Then there is nothing that cannot be accomplished because whatever is done is to the glory of God. Any soul able to commune with God is ready to manifest God.

A number of the Master's miracles were concerned with the healing of the blind. The blind represent those who lack understanding of spiritual truth. While their souls yearn for love they cannot feel it, they cannot give it. They are unaware of the invisible worlds of great beauty and radiance about them, or that they themselves live in a world which, rightly viewed, is a world of spiritual glory. What wonderful work it is to be able to open the eyes of those who dwell in darkness and show them that there is no death, and there need never be separation even when their beloved quits his or her physical body for another world! This is the work of those who have passed the Water Initiation, those who have controlled their psychic forces and who are able to see into the other worlds, those who can then convey their vision of truth to their companions.

Many people waste time and energy trying to convince others of the spirit world. There is no need to convince anybody. The best work is to give forth that power which teaches the soul when it is once ready. It is all a question of the evolution of the person concerned. There is a time for these things. Once the individual has earned the right to know spiritual truth, the teacher will be forthcoming. Sometimes men and women become excited and long to meet a master in the flesh. They are usually disappointed. But when they have at last reached the point where they are able to recognize a master, then the master will manifest. They themselves will by then have created the necessary conditions in which to receive from the master the illumination, teaching, comfort and help they require, in readiness for the next step on the path. It is a great work to restore sight to the blind; or, in other words, to be able to illumine them through the power of the Christ-spirit within.

It is not the speech, it not only the thoughts: it is the inner self of the human being that can become so powerful and so Christlike that it conveys healing, teaching, blessing. The effect of this cannot be superficial and transient, for it comes from God within the soul and is therefore eternal and infinite. Within every soul dwells God, although there are many layers to be peeled off before the Christ light can shine forth. Those who are a little more advanced than others can indeed sometimes help their brethren in the casting off of some of these outer coverings.

# 5 · The Air Initiation: 1

WHEN we speak to you we would try to raise your consciousness to the heights, for the golden circle of the Christ love is all around us. Those from the unseen world teach us not merely through words but through the language of the spirit. When we speak, a bridge between the higher worlds is built, and they can only cross it when you also ascend to the mountaintop.

It has been said that dispassion is one of the most difficult lessons for the neophyte or pupil to learn. It is so very easy to become emotionally upset by contact with inharmonious conditions or people. But as the Christ light within grows stronger it teaches the pupil to control passion and emotion, to keep it stilled and in its right place, so that it no longer storms through the person's soul, upsetting and shattering them.

So we learn through the Water Initiation the meaning of becoming still, so that the soul may know tranquillity and God under all conditions. The neophyte is calm but not indifferent; a distinction must be made between indifference and lethargy. Tranquillity and calmness are based on strength, when a clear perspective has been attained and the soul is under the direction of the Master, the Christ.

After the Water Initiation comes the Air Initiation. We have said that the four initiations—Water, Air, Fire, Earth—are not necessarily taken separately. Indeed, frequently the pupil may be preparing for all four initiations during one span of life on earth. Certainly, as soon as ever you enter upon the spiritual path, you will begin to be tried, tested and trained. During certain periods your soul may respond more readily to one of these four, in which element you may mainly work. Here we are taking the initiations separately, mainly for the sake of clarity, and to help you better to understand what is happening when you come up against them in your human relationships.

As water is symbolic of the emotional nature of humanity, so air is of the mental nature. The air element is that of the mind. We shall find that the human mind is as difficult to understand and handle as the emotions; and that just as a soul's uncontrolled emotions obstruct its development and progress, so also can its lower mind.

The object of the Air Initiation is that the higher mind (remember that there are two aspects of the mind) should take possession and become the ruler of the pupil's thoughts. They must become pure, spiritually pure, so that the mind can receive and the life become adjusted to spiritual truth—and then there is no longer conflict between the higher and the lower mind. For instance, the soul may at one time undergo a glorious and uplifting experience, and the indwelling truth in the person will assure them that their soul has indeed seen into heaven. But afterwards the soul has to return again to earth to be assailed by doubts, fears and questions. The lower mind thus becomes the tempter, doing all it can to refute, to confuse, or even to overshadow and overpower the higher mind. The higher mind receives the inspiration, the inbreathing of the air of God, but it needs to be continually fortified against the arguments of the lower mind. The neophyte has to learn that such arguments are spoken only by the mind of earth; he or she has to learn both to discern this fact, and to put this earthly mind back in its correct place!

In the course of preparation for the Air Initiation these testings will be frequent, as most of you are already aware. We would guide and help you to be very strong and to allow your intuition or your higher mind at all times to be master of the earthly mind. The former will never mislead. If you will be true to this higher mind you will obtain a wise answer to any of your problems.

It is said that Mercury is the messenger of the gods. It is also said that Mercury is the ruler of the fifth world, or sphere of the higher mind, and proceeds from higher spheres to bring truth to the earthly mind. Mercury also rules the zodiacal sign of Gemini. The symbol of Gemini, as you know, is that of the heavenly twins or the two pillars. These are the two pillars between which the soul has to pass into the temple of initiation. Shall we call one of these pillars the higher mind (which is situated at the back of the head), and the other the frontal mind, the intellect or mind of earth? In this Air Initiation the pupil has to learn true discernment in order to pass between the pillars of the higher and the lower mind. There must be perfect accord between the two. Then he or she achieves the Air Initiation.

You all experience the conflict between these two minds, these two selves. Probably your main difficulty will be to refute the telling arguments of the worldly mind, for they sound so sane and practical. There is always this pull. Do you remember the Master rebuking the wind and waves during the storm on the Sea of Galilee? He commanded the turbulent winds of the lower mind. It is of vital importance for the mind of the intuition, the mind of Christ, the mind of the spirit.

The lower mind is largely of the body, and so inherits all the attributes of death. It fears the higher mind, and would destroy the Christ in you. The story of the trial of Jesus tells how the Pharisees, or those filled with selfishness, pride and arrogance—all qualities of the lower mind—sought to kill Christ, the higher mind, because Christ stood in their way. The story of Joseph and his brethren has much the same meaning. But as people evolve and progress, their higher mind will employ the mind of earth for human benefit, instead of the earth mind trying to obliterate the higher mind. The initiate has to learn balance—that is, the lesson of equilibrium, the balancing of opposites.

Many a miracle and parable in the Bible specifially refers to this Air Initiation. There is one in which a man's right hand, here symbolic of the higher mind, had become withered and useless. The Master called forth the power of the higher mind in the man and restored the withered arm. Afterwards Jesus was chided by the Jews for healing on the Sabbath. Now the interpretation of the Sabbath day (Saturn's day) is the day of meditation and quiet contemplation of the works of God. Saturn, it is said, is a strict master and will allow no slipshod methods. No soul can pass through the ring of Saturn to enter the temple of heaven until it has passed the fine tests which Saturn sets. In other words, in true meditation the soul stands before the judgment bar, and cannot get away with anything but truth. This is why Saturn is called the 'ring-pass-me-not'. Nevertheless Saturn can be considered as the soul's greatest friend. That is perhaps why Jesus chose the Jewish Sabbath or Saturn's day upon which to heal this withered higher mind and bring it again into action.

Another parable tells how on a Sabbath day the disciples plucked the ears of corn and rubbed them in their hands, extracting and eating the good grain and letting the chaff blow away. Here the chaff represents the lower mind. The disciples, under the tuition of their Master, were able to extract truth through their higher mind, and so learned discernment and discrimination between the higher and the lower mind. All the conflict existing in the world arises between these two aspects, these two pillars.

You will see how vitally important it is to discern the difference between the promptings of the lower and the higher mind, and to think right thoughts. It is useless striving to make the outer world a better place until your innermost thoughts are true, pure and heavenly. Saints and seers and prophets and teachers of all time have learned the secret of right thought, good thought, God-thought, and they have not worried about anything else. They *become* within themselves; they are themselves lights in a world of darkness. The world may not recognize them; but always, positive and loving thoughts, kind, gentle and compassionate thoughts, radiate from them, ever helping to sow more seeds of right thought in the world about them.

All things originate from thought. God's thought created all things. All physical form is a manifestation of thought. Your world today manifests the result either of its good or evil thinking, because thought eventually creates form in matter.

We are on the cusp of the Aquarian Age, the age both of the spirit and of the mind. If the higher mind does not control the lower, then chaos and destruction will ensue—or rather, would ensue, for the higher mind is already everywhere manifesting itself. Even in material affairs men and woman are beginning to think in terms of brotherhood, are thinking how to make the world a better place, how to improve the conditions of the downtrodden. These are all good thoughts and come because the higher mind is being stimulated. Those of you who are striving after spiritual truth must learn continually to project from your heart and your higher mind thoughts of goodwill, brotherhood and love. Always see good in the ascendant, even if it appears comparatively infinitesimal. See good arising, no matter what the situation may be. Always project the light of Christ from your soul. Let your thoughts of love and goodwill be continually broadcast upon the ether. You can never know how great will be your service.

Let your higher mind dominate your life, and you will help many others along their path back to God.

# 6 · The Air Initiation: II

G OD IS ALL wisdom and love and gives to you everything you need; but it is not easy for you to have complete confidence in this divine truth, particularly when events do not unfold in a way that befits your eagerness for service. Delay is one of the trials which beset most aspirants on the path, because when the soul has seen how wonderful life may be, it longs to bring the same vision to all people. The soul feels sure that if its life were different, if some of its handicaps were removed, if only the right opportunities would come along, then at last it could render that service to humanity which it so longs to give. This period of waiting and testing is most difficult for the soul to accept with patience, because at such times the soul believes it knows best, only wishing that other people would be more receptive and open to being helped.

My brethren, let us at this moment become still in mind and spirit, and in imagination let us enter into the temple of God.... Now, as we do so, we become conscious of its radiance, and of the countless souls gathered to worship. We behold the altar blazing with light; we behold the divine Presence serving all creation at that altar. An inward voice tells us that we too have to come to receive our measure of that holy service, and in the degree that we are able to receive and absorb the essence from this divine Presence into our hearts, we become blessed with inner peace. We have surrendered all cares, frets and fevers of the lower mind, for as we meditate before the divine Presence we know that all is well.

God is all wisdom, and His–Her ways are those of an ever-loving parent, perfect and true. Earthly parents may believe they truly love, and yet will often over-indulge their child, mistaking indulgence for love. Yet the heavenly Father–Mother loves perfectly, and often wiser love causes Him–Her to withhold that which the child would grasp at and hold.

Now we catch a glimpse of the dispassionate mind, the higher mind of the divine. In a flash of recognition we are able to comprehend a love which both gives and withholds: a mind which never hurries, because it is completely sure of the outworking of divine laws, ordained to bring to the child of earth the blessing of full realization of itself and of the fullness of God's providence.

Let us bear in mind this surrender to the divine Mind as we speak of the Air Initiation. We have said that it brings recognition of and discrimination between the two minds you all possess—the earthly mind, and the mind of Christ, which is the higher or the heavenly mind. We have dwelt on the testing and the resulting conflict between these two. You know well how the so-called reason (the lower mind) can argue against the higher mind. How reasonable those arguments seem which tell us we should never let ourselves become too sentimental or idealistic; that we should always be practical and think first of our own wellbeing! Yet the mind of Christ in us reveals another, a better way of life. As long as the higher mind prevails, when we are in the temple of the spirit, it knows well enough that when we go back to the world to face all the problems of life, our so-called reason is likely to overpower us again for the time being. The task in hand is for the soul to become strengthened so that the higher mind rules every detail, and life is controlled and directed not by this so-called reason but by inspiration.

You will ask how this may be achieved. The way is by continual meditation; not only in times of quiet, but throughout your day. Go about your tasks always conscious of your higher mind (not necessarily with it at the forefront, because your earth mind has to deal with earth things; the higher mind can be imagined operating from the back of your brain). In time the higher mind will feel as though it is always there behind everything. It will become an active part of you, directing every thought and action so that the mind of earth automatically, instantly, obeys. The secret is to keep very tranquil and control the emotions. This is why the first degree of discipleship entails control of the emotional body—control of the emotions of passion, fear, despair and anger.

It means continual discipline; but if a soul will not of itself open to inner discipline, then God has to discipline the soul, perhaps through poverty, hunger, sorrow or persecution. If the soul allows the will of God within to do the disciplining, then attainment can be achieved quickly. You may think you will encounter karma thick and fast, and that it is easier to keep on jogging along and not to try to hurry your soul's evolution. But if you know that the promised land is very near and that by making an effort you can get there quickly, is it not better to make that effort, however hard it may be, than to have to endure the petty sufferings of a rebellious soul over a long period?

God is all love. God's ways, as we told you, are gentle

and kind; and if the soul is willing to open to the love of God it will be filled with all blessings. But if it is rebellious and blind, then it inevitably suffers: it bangs its head against the wall. The soul must acquire all the qualities of the Christ mind—meekness, acceptance, humility, peace—but not necessarily by the hard way! It can, if it will, learn much through happiness and joy, beauty and plenty. However, if the lessons are not learnt, then these things are taken away and the soul learns through lack of them.

Throughout the Bible many symbolic references to these two minds will be found. We are told that Moses led the children of Israel into the wilderness for forty years—a space of time symbolizing a period of waiting for their birth into spiritual life, into a promised land of light and understanding. Although the people knew that they were being led towards this land, they grumbled and complained bitterly.

Here we see the lower mind at work. Moses himself never actually entered the promised land, and few indeed of those who had wandered in the wilderness got there either. But their children entered in, led not by Moses but by Joshua. We interpret this to mean that Joshua was representative of the higher mind. You will remember that Moses was allowed to see the glories of that land from afar, but not to taste the richness of it. Is not that the way with us all? We wander for a long time in our particular wilderness, undergoing our personal testings, our course of preparation; and in due time (which may mean the next incarnation, but does not necessarily) we reach our promised land, or state of illumination, where the higher mind comes into its own, and then tastes the fruits and enjoys the wonders of the heavenly places.

Some of you are already being trained in the art of meditation. You may not yet have reached the promised land, but it is waiting; and in due time you will not only see but will actually enter in and enjoy the fruits of realization, the illumination of the higher mind.

We spoke before about the disciples plucking the ears of corn and rubbing them in their hands, so that the husks blew away and the grain was left. Even then the corn needed to be ground into flour before it could be baked into bread. The true disciple must rub away the useless husk, the material earthly things, but he or she is still left with the hard grains of corn which have to be pounded by the experience of many a life before they can become the living bread. The grinding of the corn means the working out in everyday life of the spiritual truths which the higher mind learns. The Pharisees disapproved of Jesus plucking corn on the Sabbath. Why? The Sabbath was regarded as a day of contemplation when, in the temple, in their higher mind, people took stock of their experience. To the

Pharisees religion was one thing but everyday life was another. They condemned Jesus for teaching people to apply their spiritual findings to their material life.

Elsewhere the old testament tells of twelve little loaves of shewbread [manna] which were kept in the temple. This brings to mind the twelve zodiacal experiences which every soul learns by while in incarnation. It incarnates again and again until it has accomplished what [in another tradition] are known as the twelve labours of Hercules. The twelve little loaves (or experiences) represent the sum of the human incarnations. Before they are taken into the temple they are sprinkled with incense—which means that we have to become meek enough to learn our lessons sweetly, and not in a harsh or resentful way. We must present our bread, the sum total of our incarnations, lovingly sprinkled with the sweet incense of humility so that it may be acceptable to God.

Many people, governed only by the mind of earth, say that the sermon on the mount is impractical in modern times. Yet the Sermon on the Mount is as true today as it was yesterday, and will be for ever. In it Jesus gave to his disciples, who had by now passed the first degree and were in preparation for the second, certain inner principles or rules which have to be learned and applied before the soul can be fully initiated. He divided his discourse into two parts: first stating the four aspects or four tests which every initiate would have to face; and secondly outlining the four attitudes of mind in which the candidate must accept these tests.

Two statements in the Bible would appear to be contradictory. Both concern the sermon on the mount. One reads: *He went up into a mountain and ... his disciples came unto him* (Matthew 5 : 1); and the other reads: *He came down with them, and stood in the plain* (Luke 6 : 17). Yet the two can be reconciled; because the going up into the mountain means a rising in consciousness, when the soul enters into or functions in the higher mind. But Jesus, although he had attuned himself to an exalted state in order to receive truth, had also to come down to the plain: to descend to the level of the disciples in order to speak to them at their own level of understanding. So he described the things they would have to encounter, explaining that if they accepted their testing rightly they would be blessed.

The tests he spoke of were hunger, sorrow, persecution, poverty. The tests in themselves are not so important. It is the soul's *reaction* to them, the attitude of mind adopted, that really matters; because the higher mind must govern this reaction and never the lower. If the higher mind deals with life's problems, the soul will absorb the qualities of Christ: meekness, mercy, purity and peace. It will learn to be meek in adversity, and merciful to all; it learns purity of life and thought, and learns absolute peace in surrender to God. Meekness, mercy, purity and peace are the four qualities which are essential to the soul seeking to pass the Air Initiation.

We often talk about 'sacrifice'—perhaps we use the word too much. Shall we not rather say surrender? For the soul no longer thinks in terms of sacrifice when it has become gentle, merciful, pure and peaceful. With the attainment of these qualities the thought of sacrifice fades, because the candidate has learned the lesson of divine love, and has reached such understanding and love for its brethren that its only real happiness lies in serving them. It does not serve because it is compelled to do so or because it feels that it ought to. It serves because it holds no desire to do other than to give service.

So we might say that the Air Initiation brings home the lesson of brotherly–sisterly service. The higher mind, being triumphant, enables the soul to give out of pure love for its brethren. Having learned to practise brotherhood, it has entered into the outer courts of heaven, to consort with companions of its spirit, and receive illumination from Christ, its true lord.

# 7 · The Fire Initiation

WE BRING to you all loving greetings from the brethren in the spirit life. Remember that with you, whenever you let them close, are some whom you have known and loved on earth, maybe in past incarnations as well as in the present. All through life, since its very beginning, you have been drawn into association, sometimes in great intimacy, with companions of your spirit with whom you have lived in spheres far beyond this physical plane. Let us get out of the habit of thinking of life as the short span known in one incarnation. Train yourselves to think of life as a long journey and of the many friends whom you have met on that journey being still your friends.

We say this because the limitations upon human thought have to be eliminated before men and women can live in brotherhood one with another. Imagine, for instance, as you read these words that you are free from your body, just as you are when asleep or at death (only it is not death, but an inflow of fresh life). Use your imagination to create around you a spirit temple in which you are seated. In the material world, you know that warmth in nearly every form originates from the sun. Yet there is a spiritual as well as a physical sun, for behind every physical form is the spirit, which is part of God, and which brings that form into being. Without the invisible or spirit Sun pervading the physical sun there would be no light or warmth to sustain the world. And the spirit behind the sun is moreover identical with that spirit in you which you call 'love'.

Some people mistakenly believe that love is only an emotion which you experience sometimes. No: love is the first cause of all life. Love is light and heat and life itself. This is the supreme secret which the third initiation, known as the Fire Initiation, reveals to the soul.

We have spoken of two of the great initiations. Yet we find that the Air Initiation, which disciplines and trains the mind, can still leave the soul cold—let us say, as air remains chill while the sun is obscured. We think of the mind also as being cold; for we know that intellectualism is cold and exacting, and because of this it cannot live. So the air initiate turns to something which will bring him or her warmth and life. However brilliant their mind, unless it become infused with the love of God, all its works will gradually fade and die.

It is the Fire Initiation which brings warmth and light and beauty into life. Those of you who have begun the practice of meditation have been taught to search for the spark of light within, the 'dot within the circle'. The interior of the circle may be dark, but at the central point the light is shining. You learn to focus upon that light as a first lesson in concentration.

Now many people, although they have learned to control their emotions and have disciplined and trained their minds, remain imprisoned, unable to live in the world of spirit. It is as if they were shut in a closed room, or in an iron box; and their constant heart-cry is, 'How can I become free? How can I see, live and move in a world of spirit? No matter how I struggle, I cannot break my bonds!' The reason they are so bound is that they are still striving through cold reason and logic to find their way out. This they will never do. Perhaps it sounds too homely when we say that the way to release yourself from bondage is through simple love; but this is the truth. The Fire Initiation opens the third degree of your consciousness.

In your earliest phase you are unconscious; then you become a self-conscious being; and the third degree confers upon you a measure of divine consciousness.

When this is attained, you have become an initiate of the fire element. It should be understood that all these elements operate on every plane of your being, from the lowest on earth to the highest in heaven. Love is active on all of them. On the lowest of them, you only know it as a passion that sears, burns and consumes, but on the highest plane it creates and gives life.

How can you open the door to the divine life? Certainly not by overwork on the mental plane! First you must endeavour to *feel* within yourself the attributes of Christ the Son of God: the warmth of his love for humanity, his gentleness, humility, patience and peace of spirit. Attune yourself as far as you can to the spirit of the Son of God, the lord Christ. Contemplate his nature, his brotherhood, his understanding. Dwell in his spirit. Let everything else go. You will then find that what may feel at first like a small point of light within you will expand until it becomes a golden Sun, bringing warmth. The Sun spells freedom to you. Then you are in the land of warmth and light and life.

When this occurs the vision which first opens to the young initiate is usually that of natural and rare beauty: of flowers, trees, and birds, and living, shining waters; because, as the spirit of God brought forth life for you on the astral and the higher planes. Love creates beauty on the spiritual plane. This is why those who have neglected to love others find themselves in a state of darkness, coldness and barrenness when they pass into the soul world. Love, and love alone, gives life. Only love: it does not matter in what form; only love. That which endures in art, music, literature and religion is what has been infused with both human and divine love. Other works of the human brain tend to disintegrate and disappear because they lack this quality.

The demonstration of the surpassing power of love in the story of the transfiguration is the finest, we think, recorded in the new testament, although many other illustrations can be cited. In the old testament we read of the initiate Moses and the burning bush, and later of his ascending a mountain. Now 'going up into the mountain' means his being raised in consciousness; and in that state he became so illumined, so full of fire and light that when he descended to meet the children of Israel he had to veil his face. In another passage we read of the pillar of fire by which the Israelites were led out of their bondage, away from the flesh-pots of Egypt, from material things. Afterwards they had to wander in the wilderness for forty years. So it is with some of you: you have been released from the bondage of the flesh, but are still wandering in the wilderness, and waiting to find entry into the promised land of spiritual illumination. The reference to the *pillar of cloud by day and the pillar of fire by night* (Exodus 13 : 21) means the fire of love, the spiritual light, by which God reveals His–Her divine presence to the chosen people. The luminosity of the faces of the saints is recorded throughout religion.

In Exodus we read that Moses went up into the mountain, and was in the mount for forty days and forty nights—again, the number forty, meaning the period of gestation before the full birth or the full initiation—and that when Moses ascended the mountain, fire descended upon him. This really means the rising of the creative fires throughout his whole being, a process sometimes described as fire running up the spine like lightning and illuminating the head. The dawn of cosmic consciousness means that the soul breaks its bounds and becomes united with the universal Mind. When Moses came down from the mount he *wist not that the skin of his face shone* (Exodus 34 : 29). This also is the meaning of the halo round the heads of saints: their very flesh shines with light.

Now let us consider the story of the transfiguration of Jesus. You will remember that at the time of the baptism, of the Water Initiation, the voice from heaven cried, *This is my beloved Son, in whom I am well pleased* (Matthew 3 : 17). But notice that God still withheld full authority from him at that time. At this Fire Initiation the voice added, *Hear ye him*. It was this baptism of fire which finally authorized Jesus to speak and to serve his brethren, in the name of God.

We read that when Jesus went up into the mountain—or entered a higher state of consciousness—three disciples, Peter, James and John, accompanied him. On the higher plane with Jesus appeared two initiates, Elias and Moses. Here we have the double triangle, that of the earth (Peter, James and John) and the triangle from heaven (including Jesus himself) which intermingled with the earth triangle to form the star. Now Peter, James and John, as here portrayed in the gospels, stand for the three separate qualities of faith, hope and love; the three qualities which must govern the soul when about to undergo the Fire Initiation.

When you enter upon the path of spiritual service and development, the very first quality in which you are tested, and which you will have to be strengthened to hold fast to, is that of *faith*. However difficult things are, and even if all seem to have deserted you and you stand alone, you still have to keep your faith that all is well, that you are in the care of your Father–Mother God. You must hold on to your faith that God has power to bring you through the valley of shadows, and that you are being wisely guided and led; and you have to have *hope*. Faith is an inward knowing that all is right and is working for your good; hope means an ever-growing confidence in God's wisdom, in the way you are being led.

Above all, when these two qualities of faith and hope

grow strong within, you have also to develop that state of glorious fire called *love*. Love illumines your heart and life as well as your countenance, so that light goes forth to others through your mind, through your emotions, your speech and every action. Through your whole being love flows out into the world, to touch those who are lifeless, those who are dead. Many spiritually dead people are walking your streets, particularly in the great cities, but when you have attained this Fire Initiation you will have power to bring these souls to life, power to send light to illumine their darkness, to heal their sick minds and bodies.

When the soul passes the Fire Initiation it undergoes a supreme experience which changes its whole life—as happened to Saul (later called Paul) on the road to Damascus. A great light came down from heaven and blinded him. It was a sudden illumination, a sudden overwhelming recognition of the reality of God's life and God's love.

In due time this will come to each one of you. The light will flood your being and all your gifts will be enhanced by the incoming of this divine fire, this magic, this creative power. This is the power that initiates use to perform what people call miracles, and which acts not only upon the human mind and emotions, but on matter itself. Like the old alchemy it will transmute base metal into pure gold! A transmutation such as this is the aspiration, the ultimate goal, of all brethren following the path; who seek earnestly, without thought of self, to serve their fellow beings. To serve is to love. Therefore we say, 'Cultivate the art of loving others and not yourself!' Self-consciousness is darkness. Your lower self must be put behind.

Let us consider the symbol of a lighted candle; the wick burns brightly, and little by little the wax around that flame dissolves and burns away. In a similar manner the flame of divine love by degrees consumes the lower self; it is transmuted and transformed. Love transforms life, removing all that is ugly and unwanted. What love does in life is to transform it. The transmuting power of love is the magical secret of the initiate's life. When this love fills the heart, the heart centre glows with divine fire and radiates like the Sun, and can be seen in the breast of all who have passed the Fire Initiation.

# 8 · The Earth Initiation

WE NOW TURN to the last of the four initiations: the Earth Initiation. Some believe that the Fire Initiation should be thought of as final, because in it we become consciously aware of the divine fire. But he who was called Saul, after he had been struck by the blinding light, had still to prove himself as Paul, had still to be tested for his final initiation.

The Earth Initiation is necessary because even after the soul has received divine illumination, even after it has been caught up into the heavens and seen the vision glorious, it has to learn to *use* the power of the divine fire in order to control physical matter wisely and rightly. This is what some call the secret magic. You have heard stories of adepts being able to perform what the world calls miracles; they can pass matter through matter, and can traverse great distances in a flash of time; they can produce food to feed the hungry, and can actually raise the so-called dead! Millions still doubt whether miracles such as these have ever actually happened. This is only because the ordinary mind cannot understand the process involved. We were once asked: 'If the masters are really able to feed the hungry whenever they desire, why don't they feed starving children in our midst?' A very understandable question! The masters do not miraculously produce food for the starving, for the reason that hunger is one means by which the soul, even of a child, can evolve towards divine illumination: that is, spiritual emancipation and freedom. No master, no guide, nor even an angel can do the work of regeneration for any other soul. Everyone must tread his or her appointed path from birth onwards, until the soul by its own aspiration and endeavour frees itself from the bondage of its lower nature and its prison-house of matter. The whole purpose of life is that every soul on earth may develop God-powers, and in time become a true son or daughter of a living, loving God: not a God seated on a throne in a faraway heaven, but one whose life and essence permeate every atom of creation and every vibration of a soul's inner being.

In the Earth Initiation, each individual soul has to learn that all substance is God; that everything which seems solid matter is really charged with divine energy and light. You are all enslaved in matter, enslaved by the earthly conditions which encompass you. The Earth Initiation teaches the soul how to free itself from the bondage of matter by a process of surrender which can be likened to crucifixion and death. But an earth initiate knows that there is no such thing as death. No matter how stoutly someone might believe that death ends all, and even persuade themselves that they want to die, in a spiritual sense they cannot. The candidate for Earth Initiation has not merely to accept this truth of continuing existence but to realize it within their very being—that neither their soul nor their body can ever die. The body appears to die, because the soul and spirit withdraw, unable any longer to sustain the weight and inharmony of the body; but this casting off of the body is only like the serpent shedding its skin. It is true that body afterwards disintegrates, and all its particles are dispersed; but even these particles will continue to exist in another form. The soul too continues its existence apart from the body, and eventually after preliminary cleansing returns to its true home, which is in a body of light.

More than this, if you could once realize that your physical body can be healed and protected against all harm by a shield of light, and that within you burns the divine fire of life; if you could live always conscious of this light, you would find that the very atoms of your body would gradually become etherealized. Then you would live for ever more in a body of light, although it is true that this new body of light will make little visible impression on people who are still imprisoned in matter, shut away from the light like prisoners bolted and barred in a dark cell.

What then brings about this change in the physical matter of your body? It is the action of the divine fire of love awakened by the voice of God within your innermost heart. Some would say that this voice is the I AM speaking—but you must learn to distinguish between the promptings of the personal 'I' which is of the earth, and the divine I AM, the voice of the living God—the voice divine, pure, humble, lowly, gentle, patient, kindly; the voice of Christ, the only-begotten of the Father–Mother.

What does the term 'only-begotten' mean? The term does not of course imply begotten of physical parentage but rather begotten of the Father–Mother God in the heavens. Before the earth was created—I AM! This I AM is the living and universal Christ, born deep in the cave of the heart in every one of you (in the lowly stable at Bethlehem, among the lowliest and humblest of God's creatures). It is the voice of the I AM in every heart that leads the soul, the Son–Daughter of God, through the pain and crucifixion of earth into eventual inheritance of a body of light in a world of pure light.

We are not theorizing, we are speaking of scientific truth. Your scientists already know that matter is neither fixed nor solid, and that something exists which is more real, more potent than material force and energy, which in the very core of the atom is responsible for the construction of matter. This something is spiritual substance.

After the Earth Initiation the candidate will be able to see that what is thought of as solid earth-substance is not solid at all; and that the power, capable of quickening the vibrations of matter to that point where it becomes invisible to ordinary sight, is the divine fire or light of Christ.

If you think along these lines it will help you to realize that your true state of embodiment is in the eternal light. If you cannot contact the light during meditation, it is because the lower self still imprisons you. If you will persevere in seeking the I AM, which is deeply buried in your innermost heart, you will gradually become aware of this inner spark of light. As development proceeds, you will at times find yourself enveloped in a golden radiance, and you will know the meaning of the words, 'We live and move and have our being in God'. God is our light; in God only do we truly live, and without God we have no real life at all.

So you will see that after the Fire Initiation, where the soul becomes aware of the light, the next stage must be for the soul to learn to make use of the light; and through the power of the light gain dominion over physical matter and all the lower elements of its own being and outer environment. This is the way which every soul will some day tread.

The story of the crucifixion is universal to every man and every woman, in that it explains the entire process of the Earth Initiation. Every one of you will in time become a candidate for initiation, and will go through a form of crucifixion of mind, soul or body; will suffer the pain of crucifixion, and because of this know the meaning of the resurrection and ascension of Christ. This great surrender or crucifixion applies not only to individuals but also to nations, to entire races and indeed to whole worlds. All humankind must follow the same path. Humanity must always suffer in darkness and blindness until of its own desire it surrenders self-will and becomes identified with the will of God. This will of God, working out in individual and nation alike, manifests as love, goodwill, brotherhood, justice, truth and peace.

Let us review the events of the crucifixion. From them we can learn that the divine fire was already burning in the soul of Jesus—but, as the man, Jesus had still to go through his final initiation; and as part of that great initiation he was betrayed. So also will every soul at some time know the meaning of betrayal, of being cruelly and unjustly treated. When this happens the lower self rises in indignation and demands justice. The Earth Initiation, however, teaches the soul that it is no use hitting back at anyone, and that the only way for the initiate is to forgive. Did not Jesus pray, *Father, forgive them, for they know not what they do* (Luke 23 : 34)? The awakened soul of Jesus knew that if those who tortured and betrayed him fully realized what they were doing, they could not have done these things. Indeed, no-one could ever wilfully betray or torture another if they understood the full implications of their action, or the debt that they incur. The soul of the initiate, too, cries, 'Father–Mother God, forgive them: for they know not what they do!'

Let us consider another incident which occurred during the hours of crucifixion, when Jesus called upon the disciple John and his mother Mary, standing at the foot of the cross, and said to John, *Behold thy mother!* To Mary he said, *Woman, behold thy son!* (John 19 : 25–27). The 'woman' here is a symbol of the soul; John, of the divine spirit. The deeper meaning of the incident is that the soul and the divine spirit of Jesus were at that moment merging, embracing, being eternally united. Life on earth is not finished or complete until this divine union—or, as the Hermetic philosophers say, this 'mystical marriage'—has taken place. The meaning is the same as in another parable (Matthew 25) when the soul, portrayed by the wise virgins who had made ready, went forth to meet the bridegroom.

Later, upon the cross, Jesus cried, *I thirst!* (John 19 : 28). According to the scriptures, the soldiers in attendance gave him vinegar and gall to drink: a bitter, bitter draught. But his thirst was not of the earth; his thirsting soul at that moment was calling upon the spiritual powers for succour. Nothing else could give him what he craved.

We are told that in his last moments on the cross Jesus cried out *My God, my God, why hast thou forsaken me?* (Matthew 27 : 46). Again the soul was calling upon God, because the power of the lower self upon which people usually depend was failing and departing. After the Earth Initiation the individual must solely rely upon the light and the glory of God.

Then came the cry from Jesus: *It is finished!* (John 19 : 30). This meant that he had finally overcome and was wholly master of the lower self. The lower self was dying, dead. Think for a moment of the unending conflict which goes on throughout life, between the higher and the lower. At this supreme moment the spirit of Jesus was freed, released. Had he not previously promised the thief on his right hand, *Today shalt thou be with me in paradise* (Luke 23 : 43)? These two thieves crucified with Jesus represent the higher and the lower mind. In this story the lower mind is symbolized by the thief who was debarred from heaven, and the higher by the thief who went onward with Christ into the heavens.

Then said Jesus, *Father, into Thy hands I commend my spirit* (Luke 23 : 46). This was the complete and final triumph of Jesus; and this is the final initiation for which you are all being prepared, and which you will all some day undergo. All of you will one day realize that you have always lived and had your being safe in God's life and love; that all your fears were empty, idle fears; and that the real purpose of your earth lives has been to teach you to realize your power of command over the four elements and over all matter, so that you could in the end rule as divine beings in the kingdom of eternal light.

# 9 · The Resurrection and Ascension

NEVER THINK of the spirit company for whom we speak as being in some remote place you cannot reach. The spirit world and the companions of your spirit are within your consciousness; and yet your consciousness has expanded beyond the ordinary limits of the physical senses to see them. Your own physical vibrations change when you aspire.

We must refer briefly to the problems of time and space. When we say that there is no such thing as time on the spiritual planes of existence, or indeed on earth, you will smile at us, because your clocks take their time from the sun and their hours limit your whole conception of life. In spirit there is no such limitation, because all time is at this instant! At this very instant you and we are in eternity! All that was or ever will be is existing now. Thus you may, if you wish, go forward or backward in time. Your degree of realization of the nature of eternity is all that limits you.

These words may help you to grasp that here, now and always you are enfolded in the love of the great Brotherhood. You are encompassed by a vast company of unseen companions of your spirit, some of whom you may have known and loved in former earth lives, and whom you can meet again on the plane of pure spirit. Whenever you aspire to truth, you are in contact with the age-old companions of your spirit. This means that when you have undergone the discipline necessary to enable you to become an initiate, you will know how to raise yourself to the glory of the heavens. The average person seldom thinks of their personal problems, anxieties, and even agonies as having any relation to initiation; but every sorrow, every painful experience, is helping your soul towards liberation and to realization of the kingdom of heaven, and is therefore infinitely worthwhile.

Let us refer again briefly to the Earth Initiation, for by now you may have absorbed a certain amount of spiritual understanding of these matters. You may even have glimpsed the spiritual realms and felt the presence of your guides, teachers or helpers. Yet at this point many people stop short: they know the power is available, is waiting for them, but only theoretically; when it comes to making use of this power, they fail to bring it through, or to allow the power of God to dominate their actions. Here is the secret purpose of what is called the Earth Initiation, or the ascension.

We are told that after the crucifixion, the body of the Master lay in the grave for three days, and that during this period Jesus visited souls in hell. He associated himself with his brethren who were suffering. When you yourself have passed through something which seems to you like a crucifixion, cannot you more fully identify yourself with the su erings of others? An initiate know the reason for personal crucifixion, but the souls whom the Master visited were in hell because they did not know the purpose of their suffering.

Yet you who are qualifying for initiation will know why others are suffering. You may even take the light of the spirit to souls in 'hell' to comfort them. This is work for everyone who has passed through initiation with understanding, whose eyes are opened. You can take the light of the spirit and with it comfort others. We speak most earnestly. Today millions of souls are imprisoned in darkness; only those who have seen and gained understanding of the light can comfort these disquieted souls.

After the three days in hell it is said that the body of the Master Jesus rose again from the grave. Ours is an inner explanation of the outer story. The stone which was rolled away from the grave represents the soul. It allowed the spirit of the Master to come forth. The soul no longer imprisoned the divine spirit; it allowed it to manifest, to come forth. You will remember that it was a woman at the tomb to whom the Master first spoke. A woman represents the soul too; this woman was the first to behold the Master, recognizing that she had found something greater than herself. Even during the turmoil of the outer life the soul often feels that of itself it is empty, incomplete, longing for something deeper than itself to take command, reanimate everything in life. This something is the divine spark, the pure Christ. Initiates, however, are aware at all times that they must allow this pure, this divine spark to guide and command them.

Many of you say, 'How shall I know when the voice of pure truth is speaking to me and when it is only my lower self? How shall I know whether it is my guide or the imagining of my own mind?' We answer that both mind and soul have to learn to stand aside, to become very still in order to hear the voice of pure spirit: the voice of the silence, the soundless voice which needs no words; which speaks only truth, and through which you at once know. In this way the Master in us all rises from the dead. The Master in you has arisen, or you would not comprehend these words.

After the resurrection something important follows. The Master said, Touch me not; for I am not yet ascended to my Father (John 20 : 17). Touch me not: at that moment he could not bear contact with anything worldly because he was not then complete, had not become strong enough; not yet having acquired his full glory he could be harmed by contact with the material world. Some of you will understand this feeling. You have perhaps reached and beheld the heavenly glory for a moment, and yet you are not strong enough to stand up against corruption. The material touch, you feel intuitively, might damage you.

The final test, the final experience of ascension into the heavens, is the withdrawal of the higher from the denser self, and the transmutation of the bodily atoms so that the newly etherealized body becomes established, permanent: not in an earthly but a heavenly sense. This is called the state of ascension, to which all masters attain after the highest earthly initiation. You may know that you yourself have a master. Your master will impress you with his or her presence (for the masters certainly number among them women as well as men). The ascended master, having passed this high Earth Initiation while functioning in a physical body, so transmutes its fabric into light that to the person of earth the body seems to disappear in light.

*Jesus arose from the dead!* The very atoms of his physical body were changed and spiritualized. His body became

transmuted from pain and darkness to light and freedom. Afterwards he walked and talked with his disciples
and demonstrated to the world this triumph of spirit
over matter. Then, having finished his mission, he was
enveloped in light and was caught up into the heavens.
In other words, he withdrew into that new life which
will some day come both to each individual being and
to the earth itself.

We are able to speak of what we ourselves have seen
concerning the future of humanity—of a life dawning
for men and women which can only be described as
celestial: when the light of the Son of God will shine
through their faces, when they will live without sick-
ness, pain, want or suffering, a life harmonious and
beautiful in every respect, warm and human; and where
the fullest expression of the spirit can be given. Try to
believe us if you can; try to believe that nothing is too
good to be true. Believe in God, in good!

We say that wars shall cease; that untruth and ignorance will fade away; that human life will be lived from
the centre of the Sun, from the heart of the Christ.
There will be no more deception or illusion. The whole
purpose of life here is the continued etherealization
of humankind and of the fabric of this earth. Do you
know that there are already planets in existence in
your solar system which have become so etherealized
that they are outside the range of the most powerful